IT'S A TEACHER'S LIFE

IT'S A TEACHER'S LIFE

by

David Sipress

A PLUME BOOK

PLUME
Published by the Penguin Group
Penguin Books USA Inc., 375 Hudson Street, New York, New York 10014, U.S.A.
Penguin Books Ltd, 27 Wrights Lane, London W8 5TZ, England
Penguin Books Australia Ltd, Ringwood, Victoria, Australia
Penguin Books Canada Ltd, 10 Alcorn Avenue, Toronto, Ontario, Canada M4V 3B2
Penguin Books (N.Z.) Ltd, 182–190 Wairau Road, Auckland 10, New Zealand

Penguin Books Ltd, Registered Offices: Harmondsworth, Middlesex, England

First published by Plume, an imprint of New American Library,
a division of Penguin Books USA Inc.

First Printing, September, 1993
10

 REGISTERED TRADEMARK—MARCA REGISTRADA

LIBRARY OF CONGRESS CATALOGING-IN-PUBLICATION DATA
Sipress, David.
    It's a teacher's life / David Sipress.
        p.   cm.
    ISBN 0-452-27081-2
    1. Teachers—Caricatures and cartoons.   2. American wit and humor,
Pictorial.   I. Title.
NC1429.S532A4   1993b
741.5′973—dc20   93–11015
                                                                        CIP
Printed in the United States of America

BOOKS ARE AVAILABLE AT QUANTITY DISCOUNTS WHEN USED TO PROMOTE PRODUCTS OR SERVICES.
FOR INFORMATION PLEASE WRITE TO PREMIUM MARKETING DIVISION, PENGUIN BOOKS USA INC., 375 HUDSON STREET, NEW YORK, NEW YORK 10014.

So, Ms. Miller, would you tell me briefly your methods for teaching reading, your overall philosophy of education, your views on testing, your ideas on discipline, your opinions about homework, the ways you could excite kids about science, and how you would upgrade math skills in our school should you be hired?

SIPRESS

I wish I could help you, Mrs. Rogers, but I can't read my handwriting either.
SIPRESS

Let me ask you a question about this gang that keeps stealing your homework, Howard. How much do you figure they get for a stolen book report?
SIPRESS

Psst, Marjorie, am I allowed to answer the question, "Where do babies come from?"

Alice, please! You're a practice teacher! At some point I <u>have</u> to leave you alone with them!

SIPRESS

She's been teaching too long!

SIPRESS

SIPRESS

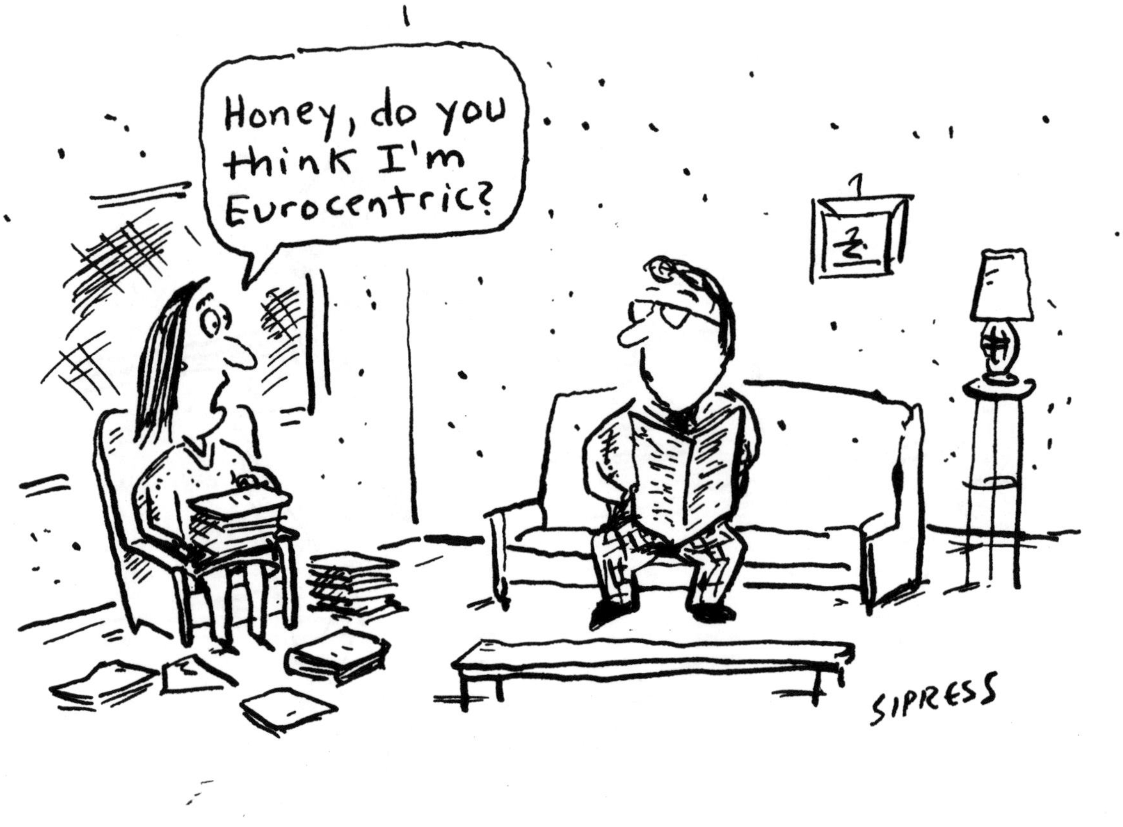
Honey, do you think I'm Eurocentric?
SIPRESS

I'm Billy's mother, and this is his attorney!

SIPRESS

Miss Rogers, Sally Green. Is it true my son's research project is "the effect of too much television on a typical ten-year-old?"

She's been teaching too long!

OK., lady, I want you to slowly hand over that purse!

Watch yourself, young man, "to slowly hand over" is a split infinitive!

SIPRESS

I'll have number four, "None of the Above."

Every year when I begin this unit on the Constitution, I feel I have to make it very clear that the Bill of Rights does not necessarily apply in this classroom.
SIPRESS

Haven't you heard, the state now mandates that students do thirty-five hours of use-ful volunteer work?
SIPRESS

There's nothing to be scared of, Mrs. Miller, it's just another teaching tool!

If I ever go to Japan, I'm sure the pilot will be able to find it, so why do I have to know where it is?

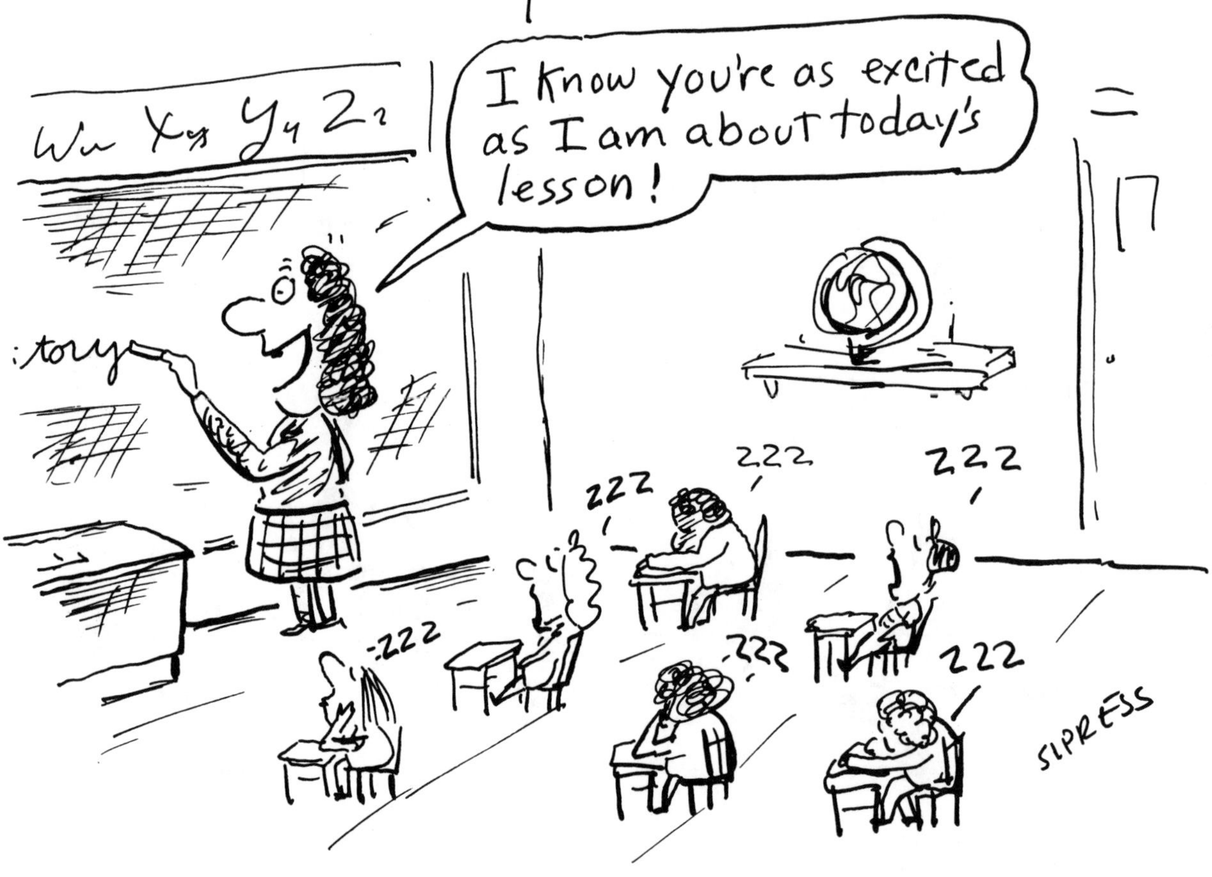
I know you're as excited as I am about today's lesson!
SIPRESS

①

What would it take to get you to do a little work, Charles?

②

Fifty bucks.

sipress

SIPRESS

She's been teaching too long!

SIPRESS

That's ex<u>cellent</u>, Caroline!

Roger! Put that grenade launcher away immediately
or I'm going to have to report you to the principal!

Let me tell you, Kittles, after a hard day's work there's nothing I like better than to sit in my favorite chair, eat left-over Chinese food, grade 72 math tests and read 50 English papers.
SIPRESS

SIPRESS

SIPRESS

About the Author

David Sipress is the author of
It's a Mom's Life, It's Still a Mom's Life,
It's a Dad's Life, It's a Cat's Life, Sex, Love, and Other Problems,
and The Secret Life of Dogs. A cartoonist and sculptor,
he currently resides in New York City. His work
has appeared in Spy, Harper's, New Woman, Family Circle,
Psychology Today, and the Boston Phoenix.